**CURNOW**
**INSTRUMENTAL**
**PLAY-ALONG**

# PIANO ACCOMPANIMENT

# FIESTA

ISBN 978-1-4234-6786-1

**CURNOW®**
**MUSIC**

EXCLUSIVELY DISTRIBUTED BY

**HAL•LEONARD®**
**CORPORATION**

7777 W. BLUEMOUND RD. P.O. BOX 13819 MILWAUKEE, WI 53213

In Australia Contact:
Hal Leonard Australia Pty. Ltd.
4 Lentara Court
Cheltenham, Victoria, 3192 Australia
Email: ausadmin@halleonard.com.au

Visit Hal Leonard Online at
**www.halleonard.com**

# CHIAPANECAS

PIANO ACCOMPANIMENT

**Mexican Folk Song**
Arr. **James Curnow** (ASCAP)

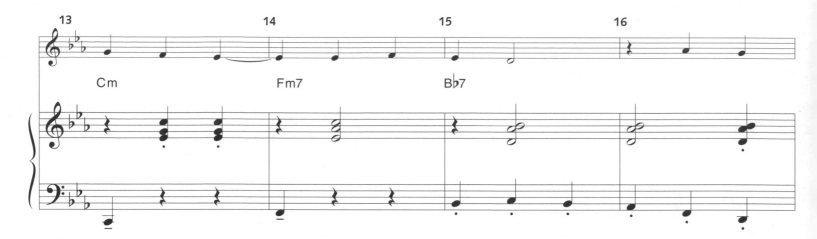

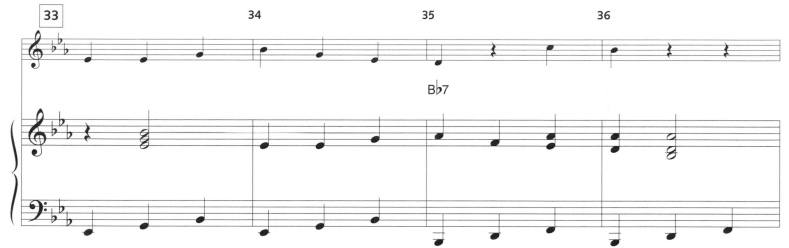

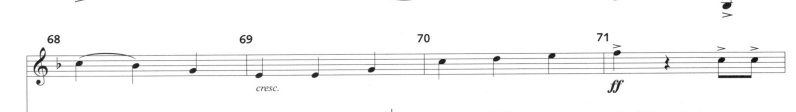

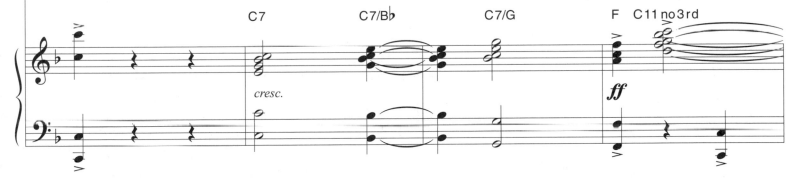

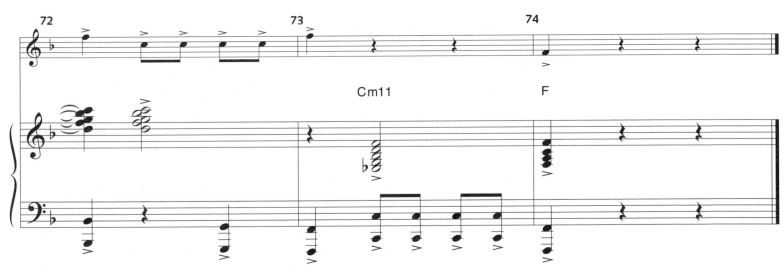

# HAPPY YULE
## (Feliz Natal)

**Brazilian Folk Song**
Arr. **James Curnow** (ASCAP)

PIANO ACCOMPANIMENT

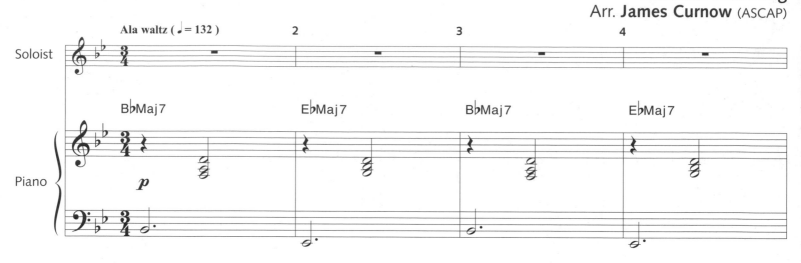

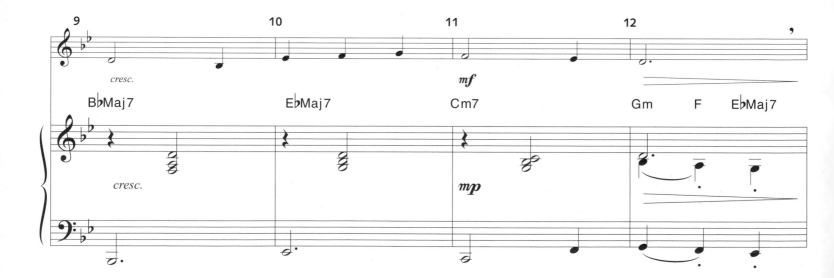

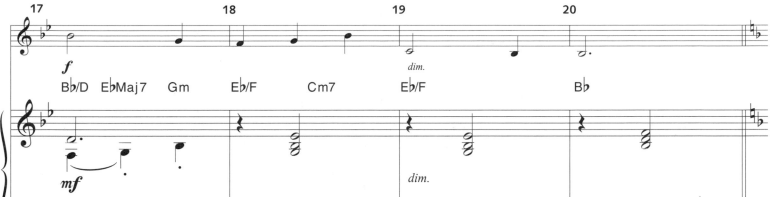

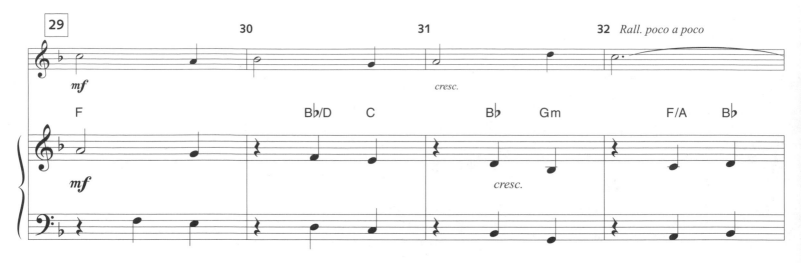

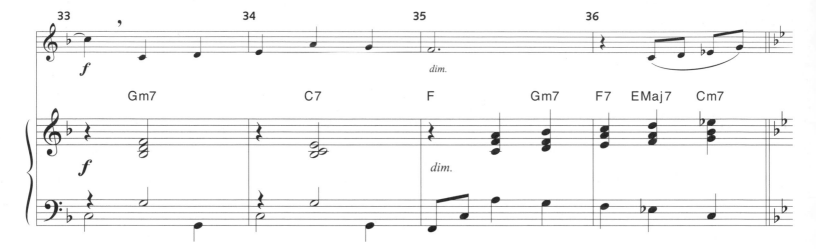

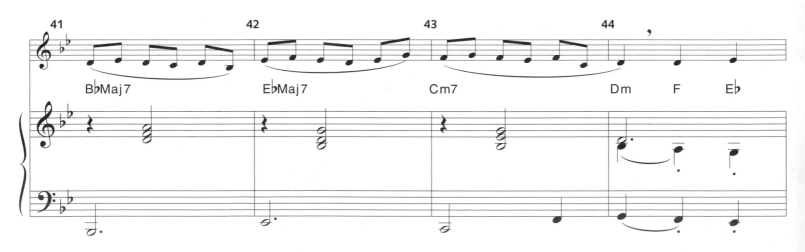

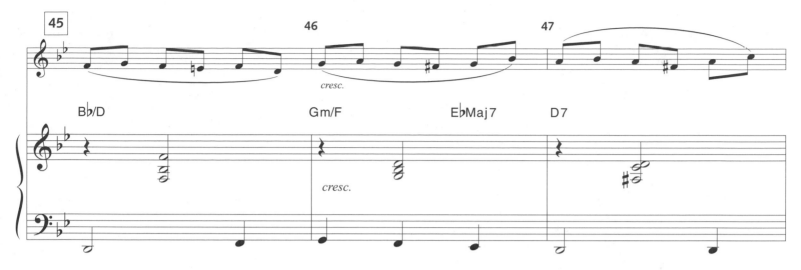

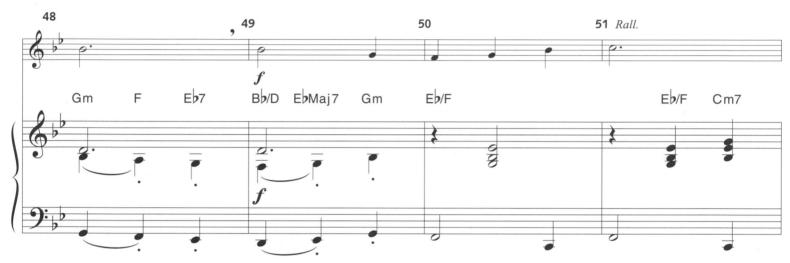

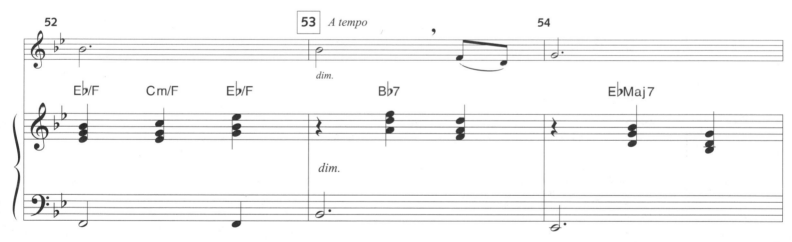

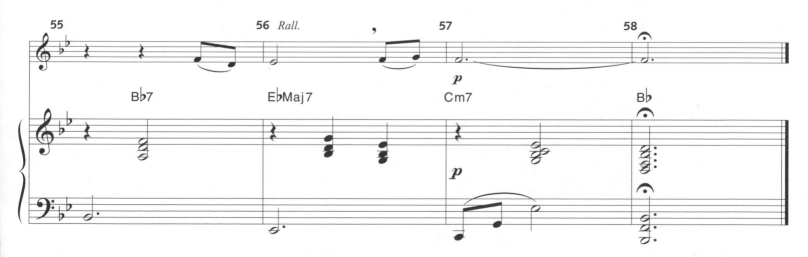

# MORNING SONG
## (Las Mañanitas)

**Mexican Folk Song**
Arr. **James Curnow** (ASCAP)

PIANO ACCOMPANIMENT

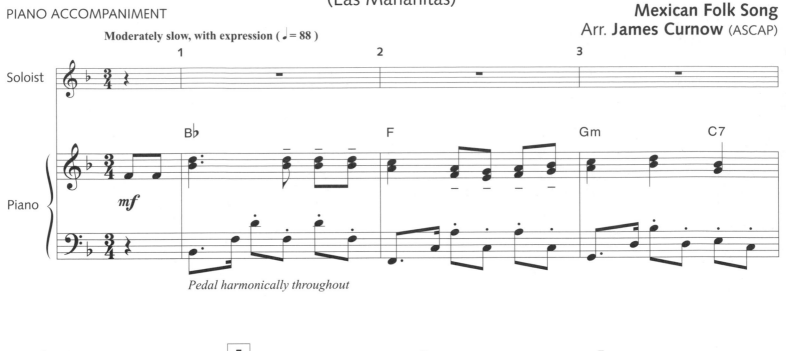

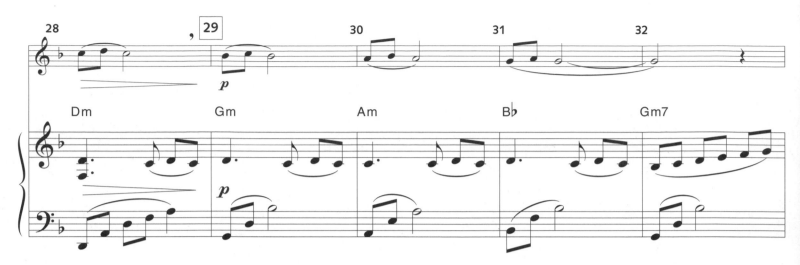

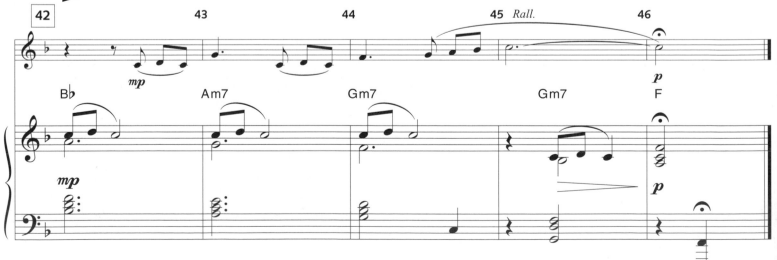

# CARMELA

Spanish-American Folk Song
Arr. **James Curnow** (ASCAP)

PIANO ACCOMPANIMENT

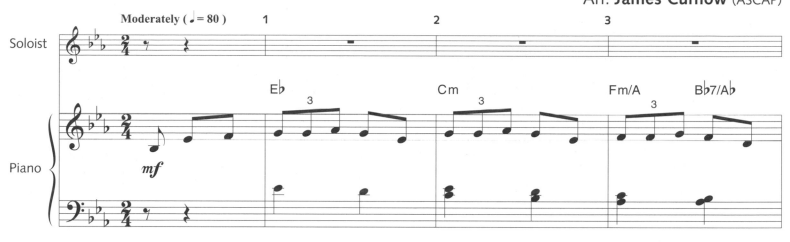

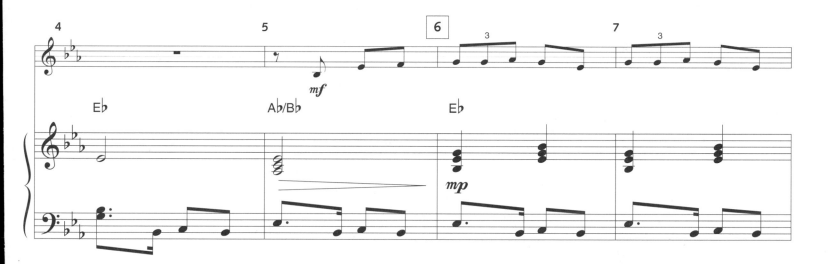

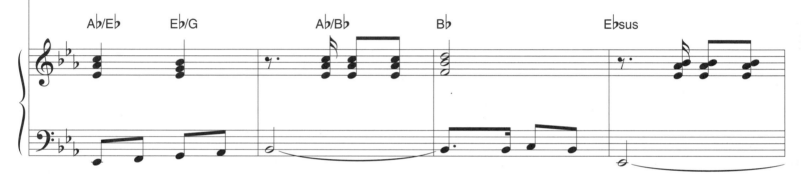

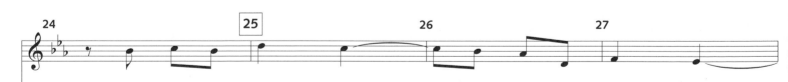

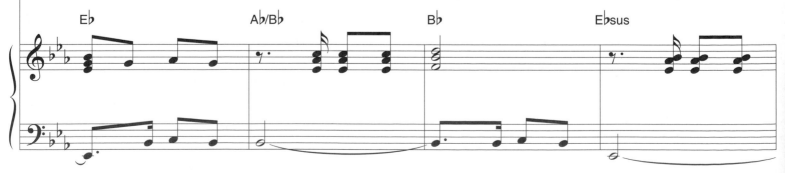

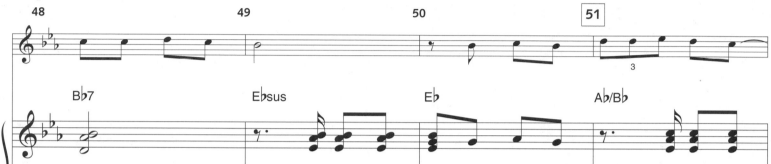

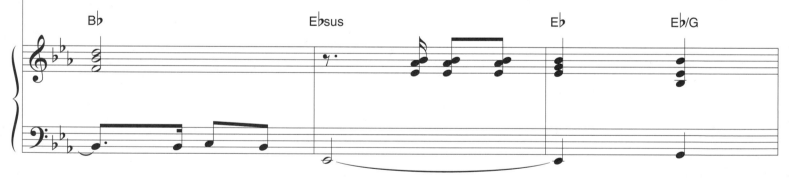

# CIELITO LINDO
## (My Pretty Darling)

PIANO ACCOMPANIMENT

Music by **C. Fernandez**
Arr. **James Curnow** (ASCAP)

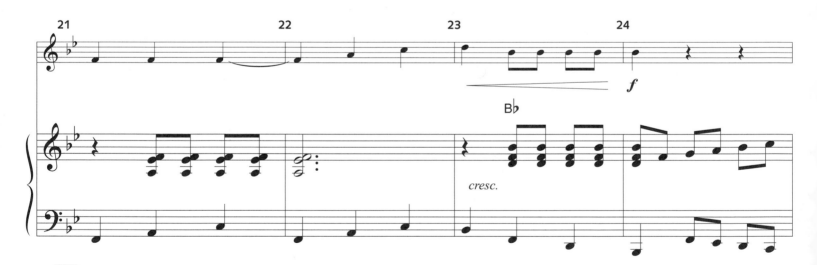

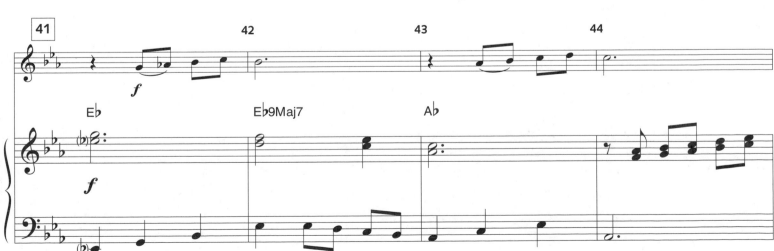

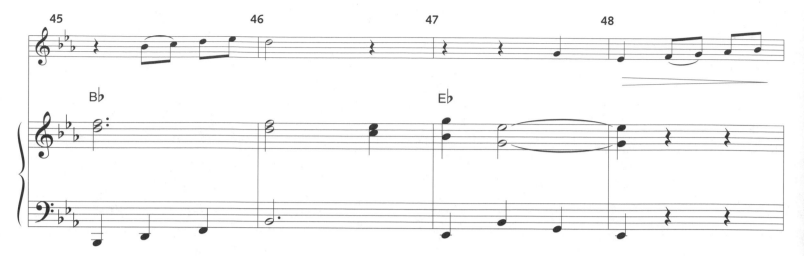

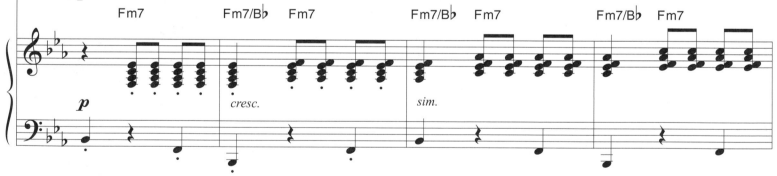

# LA PIÑATA

**Mexican Folk Song**
Arr. **James Curnow** (ASCAP)

PIANO ACCOMPANIMENT

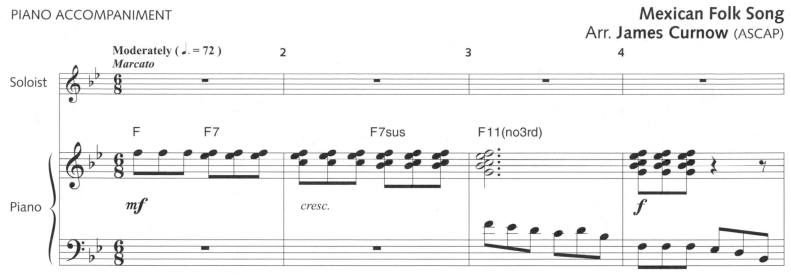

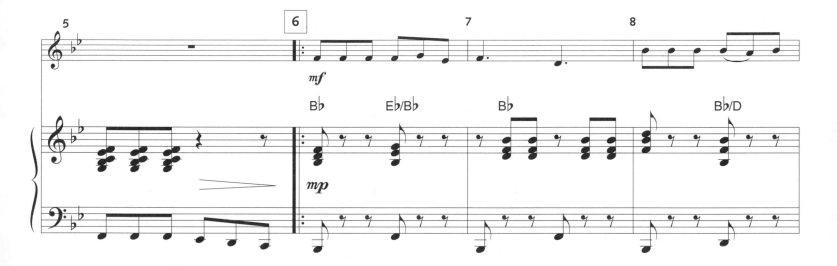

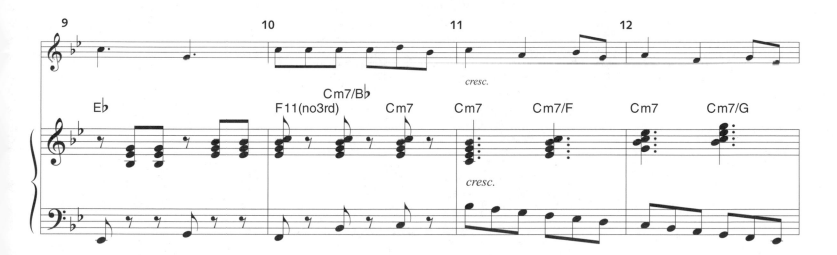

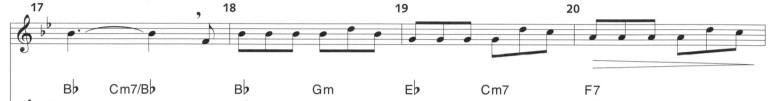

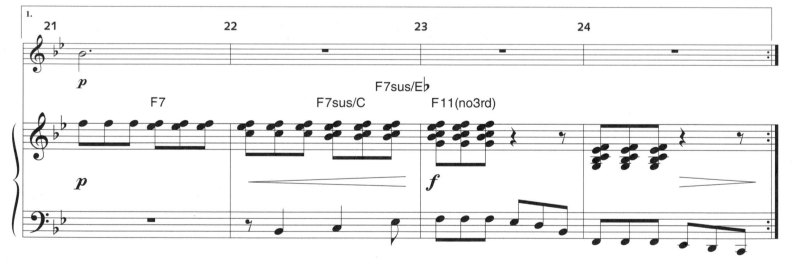

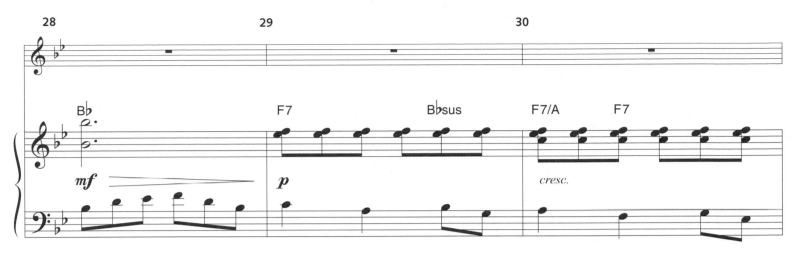

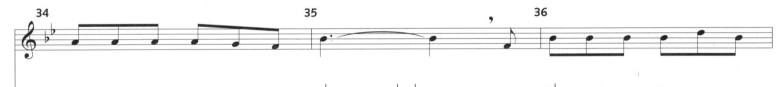

# RIQUI RAN

PIANO ACCOMPANIMENT

**Latin-American Folk Song**
Arr. **James Curnow** (ASCAP)

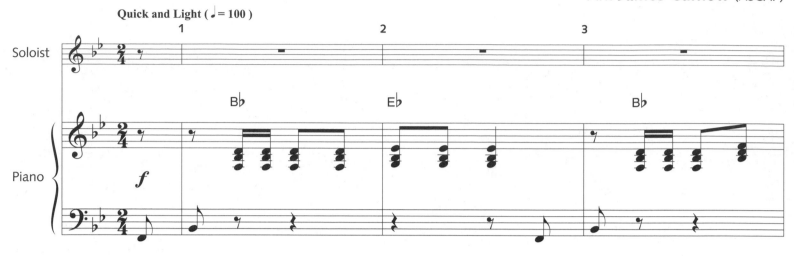

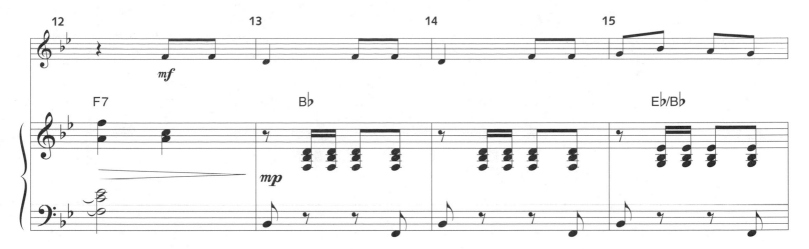

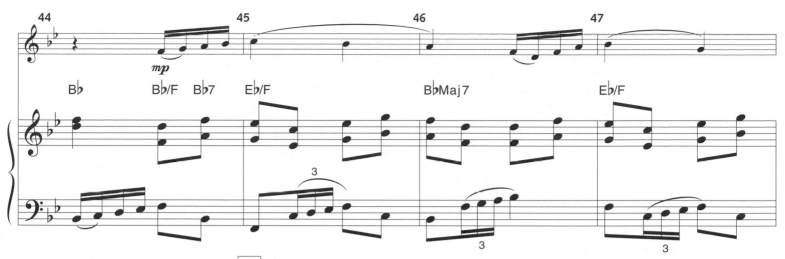

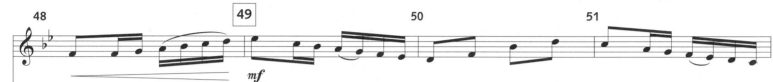

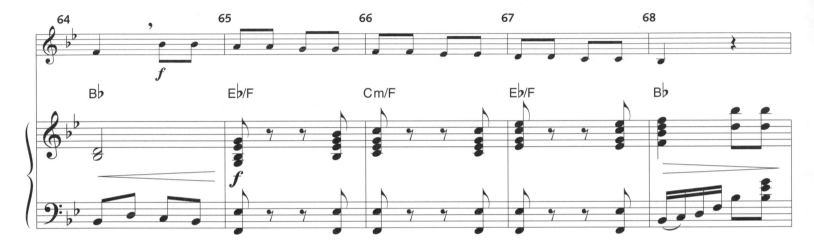

# ASK OF THE STARS
## (Preguntales a las Estrellas)

PIANO ACCOMPANIMENT

Mexican Folk Song
Arr. **James Curnow** (ASCAP)

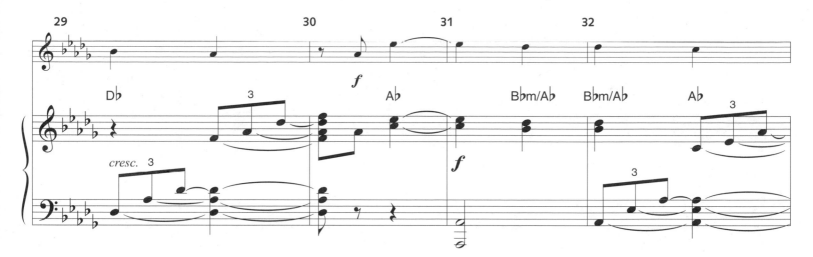

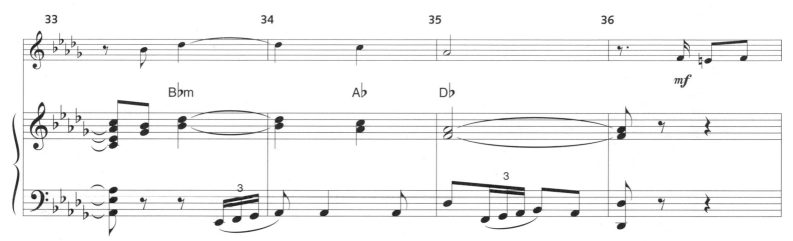

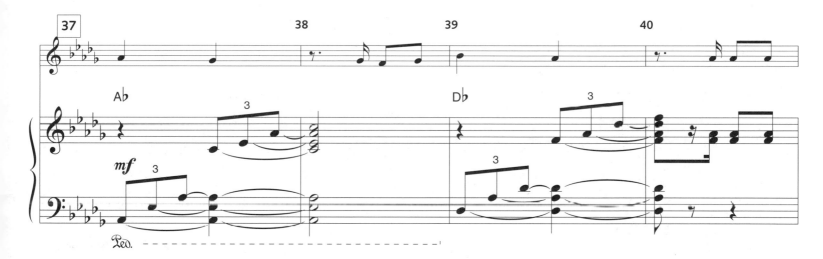